916 £1.

Jenny Morris was born in North Yorkshire and spent some of her childhood in Scotland. She writes poems and fiction. Her writing has been published in the UK, USA and Australia. She has lived and taught in Norfolk, Dorset, Sussex, Kent, Surrey, Wiltshire, Hertfordshire, London, Germany and Singapore.

A sequence of her poems was awarded first prize at the Writers Inc Writer Of The Year competition in 2002 and she read these at the Barbican. Two years later, in 2004, a short story of hers was also a Writers Inc winner. Her poems and short fiction have been recent prize winners in the Ver, Envoi, Literary Review, Aberystwyth, The New Writer, Faber And Faber, Avalon, Barnet and Pitshanger competitions.

Her previous two poetry collections are 'Urban Space' and 'The Sin Eater'.

LUNATIC MOON

Jenny Morris

Jenny Morris

Editors:

Tom Corbett
Helen Ivory

Assistant Editor:

Ian Buck

Production Team:

Jude Sayer
Lee Seaman
Catherine Taylor

GATEHOUSE PRESS LTD

Gatehouse Press Limited
Gatehouse @ Cargate Lane, Saxlingham Thorpe
Norfolk NR15 1TU

Gatehouse Press Online At:
www.gatehousepress.com

First Published in Great Britain by
Gatehouse Press Limited 2006

Printed and bound in Great Britain by
Biddles, King's Lynn

ISBN (10 Digit) 0 9554770 0 X
ISBN (13 Digit) 978 0 9554770 0 3

Cover design by Jenny Morris and Lee Seaman

With thanks to everyone involved in the production of this
book.

For Charlotte, Maisie, Henrietta,
Harry and George.

CONTENTS

ALTAR TO THE UNKNOWN GOD

This is for you. Written words left out.
Oak leaves caught the early light,
watched you, green eyes in trees
on those North York moors.
Your time drained away until insects
nested in your hair and those
foreign leaves rose from your eyes
under the earth.

On this side of darkness
empty wings beat in the woods
by the brick ponds. Your dream head
a paper lantern glowing in my night.

Your boy's life glimpsed through photographs,
sfumato, cocooned in your father's
summerhouse as an amber fly.
Round eyes over your infant's mug
of goat's milk. Your cloth doll swung by its feet.
Round glasses hiding that sad look,
a shyness. Sent away young to the choir school
in Low Skellgate. Such neat hair,
shining smile, a preciseness.
You held up the pumpkin as an offering.

I hold your afternoon photos of Karachi,
note your interest in bazaars, mosques,
palaces, camel carts, water wheels, beggars,
scribes, knife grinders, a small man
skinning a kid.

Kindness follows you around.
Your books, annotated in tiny script,
line my walls. That black silk gown
with silver daisies you gave your mother –
I wore it to shreds.

After the dregs of the day you learned
loneliness, secrecy and despair.
Did the leaves whisper warning signs?
You saw gaudy muslins, crumbling towers,
bursting fruit, flesh, a triangle of sky,
rain and tumbling stars. You heard
nightmare wings rustling and scented almonds.
You chose to die without explanation
and slipped away, silent in Delhi,
city of the shadowless djinns.

TO DO WITH ARCHAEOLOGY

My father kept a secret skull
concealed in paper, under shoes.
An ancient, dark, old dome that grinned.
My little brother found it once
and cleaned its teeth with his small brush.
Our mother caught him in the act.
The bathroom echoed with her screams.
"I didn't use that brush of yours,"
he said. But she was so outraged
she swore she'd chuck "that dirty thing"
that cranium, straight in the bin.
(My parents' interests were diverse).
The skull just vanished after that,
was never mentioned any more.
I hope it rests in peace somewhere.

ALMOST WINTER

Autumn morning
in a country churchyard
clutched by drystone walls.
Rooks flap and flag
through mist and shadow.
Blackberry gems spike
broken headstones
moss and tall weeds.
My octogenarian father searches
for his father's burial place
hidden in this desolation.
Without his stick he stumbles
over knee-high tussocks
and stretches his length
in a stranger's grave.
Unable to pull himself up
he lies helpless,
white hair shivering among
cobwebs and wet grass roots,
his blue eyes holding only
a glaze of fear.

WANTING TO DO DIFFERENT

She wrote words back to front at five.
So REFINNEJ and TERAGRAM
were hers, a magic cryptogram.
Her names made foreign helped her thrive.

She lived her life a bit like that
And thought straightforward folk were fools.
In different ways she broke all rules,
that odd and dreamy flitterbat.

She listed things no-one could see,
drew shells and stars from inside out.
When viewing wonders, she'd no doubt
that transpositions were the key.

And when she left the final town
to drown in air or burn in seas -
her searching soul somewhere at peace -
they hung her paintings upside down.

REPEATING MISTAKES

All my travelling and nothing to show for it
but an inheritance of thin legs and dark eyes
that stare from long ago photos, the same
tiny handwriting annotating old books.

We live the same lives over and over
making errors - driven by desire or grief
choosing the unsuitable mate with bitter
moods, no socks and garlic hatred.

We recede, determined not to make
a fuss about food choice, draughts
and pot-throwing in the pantry. Tense
we shake a foot like a rattlesnake's tail.

Our words breed and blossom and spread
like Russian vines, covering old bones
man-traps and deserts. Ancestors' words
echo in our mouths and we repeat their mistakes.

We love and pity the grandfather who talks
to his cabbages, the penned-up infant with no
picture books. Without pity there can be nothing
but people who resemble gravel or dust.

CHINESE DISH

A milky glaze smooth
over two filmy fishes
in shades of blue,
fins flowing together
over the weighty crazed bowl.
Each fish with its own
characteristics.
One with dominating bulk,
one submissive-eyed,
entangled, swimming together
yet apart.
Because it was important
a symbol of something
in a rage he chose it,
hurled it at her
to smash against the wall.
Silence. And the children's eyes
round like the fishes' eyes,
blue goggles in whiteness.

GIVING UP ON PAINTING THE TOWN RED

Light struggles through mulberry glass.
Sour cranberry taste floats
in your mouth like regret.
Above, the globe revolves, fractures
pieces of fire to a shoal
of ever-changing gleams.
You hold that clouded sourness
on your tongue as metal.
The music's a giant heartbeat in the dark.
You feel your blood surge
Through your limbs in time
to the clash of cymbals and saxophone.
Reflected in a window you see
someone not in this world
and you are not surprised.
It is the wrong side of night.
Discs of silver infect you from above.
As you hold the tainted glass
the tart cranberry tang
is slight enough but strong enough
to destroy any small pleasure.

IN VINO VERITAS

The caged bird never sang in there,
drab curtains drawn, the fire weak.
The woman chose her words with care
her husband stared, would seldom speak.
Their daughter left to drift abroad
to risk her soul, to ride the wind.
Her parents' dreams passed unexplored.
Their lives were always disciplined
as chained together, occupied
with spinning out each threadbare day
their discontent intensified.
They opened wine one Christmas day
and drank it with unpractised grace.
The fire died, the rain began
when, maudlin, fond, she stroked his face.
"I never loved you," said the man.

PAINTED WOMAN

This silver platter's heavy
with John's head in a pool
of dark blood which stains
his beard, drips over the lip.
I have to hold it away from my skirt.
Dish-dead he looks me in the eye
as if he understands. More than
my erect stepfather with his smirk
and confused smoke white hair.
Under her hood Herodias
takes stock, she won't lose her head.
Vicious, nagging old bitch.
Perhaps now she'll be satisfied.
Finally I've done the right thing.
Pleasing the old man is essential
for a girl in my position.
Flames light up my night
as I shimmer in my Venetian red dress.
We're all shades of scarlet here.
That stupid dancing's hateful,
moving my hips, uncovering myself.
Pour more wine for heaven's sake.

NATASHA AND THE BIRDS

Like dead fledglings, she thinks,
plump stippled corpses of dropped
hibiscus flowers
clammy, purplish, veiny.
Can't pick them
off the floor
because her flesh creeps.
Natasha from Georgia
makes men pay, never lets them
kiss her on the lips,
blocks her chimney in case
a bird comes down,
won't walk near pigeons,
remembers her mother's hands
fluttering behind bars.
Natasha, marsh mallow woman
never puts silent trumpets
of hibiscus in her hair.

MY LADY OF THE PAVEMENT

Midge was a wonder among the freaks:
glass-eater, armless woman, dog-faced boy,
jelly-man, girl with the pickled head.
Midge laughed with the imposter cripples,
palm-readers, dingbats with tertiary syphilis.
Humpty Hunchback was her man, watched her
as she cruised Seven Dials, worked
the streets, brought joy. She was a marvel among
the human pincushions and tattooed crowd.
She was a tobacco flower, heavy-scented,
a bell-shaped blonde, showy only
where moonlight leaked. He waited
in the dark, said, "My lady of the pavement,
her heart in her handbag. She's all mine."

THE GRAVEDIGGER'S WIFE

Sky curdles. Light drains out. Leaves rot.
My spade handle's broken, digs

in my flesh. Pain spikes my palm.
My boots stamp down. Toecaps

ring against metal. Heavy black
earth sticks with decay, is hard

to lift. Dug shards and spoil
make a cairn to shut out yews

and tombstones. All's darkening.
I grub, gouge deep, a measured length

and width, a certain depth.
Weary, I unbend to look up.

A rectangle frames my life.
There are more stars up there

than a gravedigger can count.
Gleaming, fading and passing.

She'll lie here tomorrow without me.
Still. Only moving in dream

and memory. Lamplight of my dusk.
Who knows that underground

sliding, creeping creatures don't sing
a sort of requiem? Make harmony.

Something always comes of something.
An earth change, a spell with rain and sun

and this small matter's altered.
Pale green blades, flickers of life

will shoot. In the spring I'll sit here
among the flowering amaranths

and my hand will be healed.

FIXED AND FALLING

Grinning in sealed landscapes
old photo figures are glued
down. Black, white, sepia.
Mouthing crucial words.
Grit in the timer shifts
grain by imperfect grain
while no floating bones
unwind the night.
When the sun flares near
rips through shadows
makes them smoke
she slams the shutters.
When wind fumbles the latch
and muffled wing beats
sound outside each window
she doesn't care to hear.
Her roof weighs no empty sky.
Inside candles gutter.
Wax drips, solidifies
as pain clogs limbs.
She will be stuck down
like that.

WATER SHADOWS

Wet coils loop, withdraw,
conceal reflection.
All familiarity spliced.
Her face suspended
interrupts into spare shapes.
Random eyes skew,
doldrum smile unwinds,
features meander out of kilter
through unfurling threads of hair.
Shivering mirror image
disintegrates entirely.
She can't put it together again.
Kneeling on the river bank
Ophelia, disturbed,
sees herself
drifting apart.

PROSPECTS

Old mensch moulders in a tenement.
His head must-stuffed
his seized joints shackles.
Each morning a slow, crutched
negotiated toil to a window.
Only a view of bricks, engravings
of close walls and passage end.
Baked clay lines, intricate textures,
irregularities yield interpretations
in the filtered, sullied shining.
Lamplighting images change with time,
fuse shades and seams in soot.
As if fire watching, he reads
sights in the walls; secret symbols,
profiles of loved and unloved women,
Corinthian pillars, sly fish,
men in wigs, rearing horses,
tulle cliffs, sparrowgrass,
angels, dumplings, bagpipes,
wigwams burning on the prairie,
clothes peg gipsies, gibbets,
a bratwurst and a tattered shroud.
Each day knucklebone fears
are stamped before his eyes.

OUT OF THE FOREST

No happy ever after
in her case. She followed the North Star,
animal tracks, trod winter glades,
hearing a distant echoing cough,
feeling his presence near her small,
small bones. Not that she was averse
to the errand. Blood's thicker
than ice. But she had no nursing skills,
just liked the colour of holly
berries, was dutiful.

After, she stayed at home,
gained weight, shambled in nightwear,
swallowed potions, blamed her mother's lack
of specific warnings, had the dog
put down. His long wet tongue
and slavering jaws reminded her
of the beast in the wood, the day
she took a basket and what great fears
she had to her grandmother's.

CHILD AT A FESTIVAL

I ride from the gloom
on a broken-backed horse.
His ribs in my flesh,
his lungs ratchet and wheeze.

A wing of mine's lost
fallen down in the dark.
This one, like a hand
waves at every response.
I don't understand
what the question might be.
Its white feathers spike
as my fingers could do.

My hair's filled with discs
of false daisies and pins
that stick in my head.
And my fist's in my mouth
to stop all the words
that might drop in the road.

We hobble and clunk
towards people at dusk.
We're looking for light
just to show where we are
and why we are here.

VISITATION

A weighty flutter overhead.
An owl comes out of the night
moves through darkness to settle.
Donna La Morte whirrs down trailing
feathers like shroud garments.
Turns, her beak becomes fleshy lips.
She speaks lies in a language
I don't want to understand.
She holds up a mask to hide her skull.
A stiff white Venetian face,
almond spaces curved in gold.
Black holes in her head.
She is all brocade, lace, gauze
sequins and silver flowers.
She is all Carnival, insincere.
I attack her in silence.

FIGURE WITH ONE HUNDRED STICKS

This old bone peasant
the size of my thumb
has broken feet, discoloured
veins down his legs.
He treads an ancient circular path.
On his back a wood bundle
of weighty toothpicks
braces him upright.
His arms fold into the delicate
shining curves of his robe.
In some lights, his stoic
white face smiles.
He doesn't hold oriental
banners of resignation.
Age destroys. Age destroys.
His burden gets heavier daily
with dust.

EMMELINE IN WINTER

She saw the Fair across the fields
was pulled in to foreign scents
tangerine clouds of candy floss
scarlet blare of saxophones
a calling drumbeat, gun shots
purple tinkling stars, flares and acid
yellow screams of fun and risk.
Hesitant, open-mouthed
she was whirled around, disgorged
too late for sense.
Then home by the back lane
and the clock unstopped, grate cold.
She was tied to the bedpost
battered with her stepmother's belt.
First light she stirred
limbs pale as peeled twigs
but soft, with risen bruises
like familiar faded tattoos.

WHAT THE DWARF SEES

The night sky is a rock wall
with stars sparking footholds
he could climb, treading on glitters.

This sorceress moon smiles
down at him tonight, singles
him out, at his small window.
He must tell his stepmother.

Her dandelion clock head looms,
booms, "You're talking with parsley.
Garnishing things. Telling lies, boy."
She has machine-gunner's eyes.
He studies the floorboards.

Reinventing himself, he looks up.
The moon smiles at him again.
His crisped mouth opens and shuts,
sounds bubble out like stones
dropped down a well.

In his mind he runs with his whacking
bladder. Thinks: She'll never see what I see.
May the moon strike her dumb.
May the sky fall on her with its rocks.
May the wind howl in her skull.

A SISTER'S STORY

When I went to pick mushrooms,
I passed my baby brother on the step, grave,
putting beech leaves on his head.
He waved. Our house was a grey lump
midden like. Hare hung from a doornail
by bloodied fur. The sky
a heavy lid lowering a swollen sun.
Trees dripped. Mist threaded pine needles,
shrouded yellow chanterelles.

When I returned cold
with my hirpling father
the soup smelled good
thick herby leveret fragrance
simmering on the fire.
My stepmother showed her axehead
teeth, dished it up.
We made to devour.
"Where's wee lad?" My father's moustache
glinted with broth.

Then we saw in her ladle
a small foot. In my bowl tiny fingers
floated to the surface.
Scent of fear in the room. Gagging.
Hinges creaked like my father's curses.
At once the moon was a skull
coffined in our windowpane.
Soon the devil will swing
through my stepmother's bones.

LUNATIC MOON

Light leaks through this wall
killing shadow dreams
where my lilac mother floats.
She knocks on my heart.
Moon dust falls on her face
spoiling her violet smile
and filmy fingers.
I must lure her back
out of the night,
my true mother who faded
into bones. Her honey hair
fell down. She called
like a raven until
her breath stopped.
And then the false mother
came with her jangles,
manic lies, closing the door
on my father's voice.
Bruised moon falls
over the edge.

ABSINTHE

The death bird screamed.
Mountains were granite.
Your mother lay on a bier.
You were struck dumb,
a bone-faced mime
tasting wormwood.

The other one came later.
You weren't of her blood,
no fruit of that sour womb.
The climate was always harsh.
Silent, you tried to squeeze
attention from your father.
He only rattled, wasted.
You kept mum, shrivelled.

You drink green absinthe
in long nights. Your
bottled madness.

You are secret. Take risks.
Open the doors. Let the lies out.
Your unspoken words must escape.
You will fall from everlasting
cliffs because of this.

MICROCOSM

Your pale eyes,
glass stones
are cold to me.
Shuttered face,
hard stare
as hands work.
Imprison yourself
in miniature.
Child who eats blooms,
you look like your kin.
My heart won't
warm to you.
Not of my blood.
Say not one word.
I take the whip
from the wall.

STAMMERING BOY, AWAKE.

Starshine leaches through a window
between dangling curtains on their gibbet,
makes milk daubs on a barred bed
where a small face watches the dark.
Faint light seeps from a door crack.
He can't speak without stuttering
and only wants unbroken words.

Night is in his room, surrounds
him with its tight closeness.
Fear blocks his stumbling tongue.
That black shape in the corner
moves towards him with a rustle.
It's the hooded hagwitch emerging
from the cupboard, her long arms hanging.

He senses her creeping closer
making it painful for him to breathe.
Silence. Clouds cover his small sky.
He feels her fitful hair touch
his face. He wants to scream
but his mouth's a soundless pit.
A weight on his chest pins him down.

Like a spider spinning a cobweb
his false mother moves her silky threads
back and forth over his skin.
He knows that she's a loom weaving a spell
to kill him. A cocoon, he can't move.
She's his night hag who stops his stammers.
Stops him ever speaking again.

INFANT IN THE STEPMOTHER'S GARDEN

The gate to the wood is chained
and lacquered fish mouth warnings.
Beyond the stile and cedars
his thistledown head is dwarfed by grass.
He follows yew roots sliding loose
in the purple shadows of topiary,
investigates ladybirds hunting
on the undersides of box leaves,
touches with his pale eyes
stone fruit dripping swags
of petrified foliage,
collects wooden roses of cones
and negotiates cobbles leading
to tiger lilies, acanthus spikes
and terracotta jars.

Inside the great hazel hedge
he is lost in darkness
below cypress sentinels.
Now his inquisitive smallness
must test the deep murk of the far lake
while on the empty croquet lawn
there is no thunk of mallets
to disturb the hot silence.

STEPSON

Someone follows me.
I turn and no-one's there.
Daily I sense him
with his olive throat, Greek
profile and jutting chin.
His presence on an empty road
and birds calling in the cypress trees.
I did wrong, no doubt.
Others suffered for my pleasure.
They said, "Wine's in, wit's out".
It was never like that.
But a sober passion, a drug.
The short nights unwound
round the curve of our hearts.
He was a man like no other.
No, that's not true.
Naturally he was like one other,
his father, my husband. Same
long bones, deep-set eyes with a glint
of dark glass. I was mad for him.
Witless, and wine poured out with the blood.
I'll be on my own forever.
Who shadows me?
Are the doves singing
or mourning?

MRS POPPLE IS VIGOROUS AND UPRIGHT

Fuchsia bells toll
in my head. Susceptible to whitefly.
Sun arrows on these showy shrubs.
Like a red blossom moving
to another's tune, I feel hollow.
These children mean zilch to me.
I'm not susceptible to them.
Throw glass beads at them and they howl.
What does it signify?
Unwashed, they keen all day,
wallwailers making silver stains.
I leave the door open
to let the sound out.
Try on my iron shoes. Trap up and down.
The sky curdles its purple petals.
I stare at the horizon.
Block my ears. Think of the sea
unwrinkled, awaking, washing
everything away.

KAREN'S SONG

The scarlet shoes must cause me pain.
I wear them when my mother dies.
I dance and try to stop in vain.

In church they glow like plums. Profane.
They're unrestrained. They scandalize.
The scarlet shoes must cause me pain.

I'm proud, bewitched. It's very plain
they fit me well. A dazzling prize.
I dance and try to stop in vain.

The soldier nods. I can't refrain.
The angel looms to moralize.
The scarlet shoes must cause me pain.

The axeman with a sharp disdain
must hack my ankles down to size.
My bloody shoes dance off in vain.

With crutches next I try again
on wooden feet, a sad disguise.
The scarlet shoes have caused me pain.
Such agony for being vain.

PEEP SIGHT

He jumps up, black
jack-in-the-box,
huge, hurtling words.
She wants to see him small,
framed and distant,
a target aligned in that
tiny round eyehole.
She wants to hold him
as an image in her head,
shivering as on a pin,
unable to spring and tower.
She wants to put the lid
on him forever.
Her witchy hands grip
the enforcer as at last
he becomes trapped
in her range.
Now she has him
in her peep sight.

TENSE SITUATION

She was a woman with a past,
active in her doings,
living for the present
(or presents, definite articles).
She was superlative,
the object of his affection.
There was no comparison.
His was the passive voice,
reflective, negative,
subject to her wishes.
His was the possessive case,
sometimes interrogative.
Hers was imperative, conditional.
But the imperfect past
of that singular person
always got in the way.
Their future was indefinite.

ARIZONA PROSPECT

This old photo pulls me in, keeps me out.
Cloud-filmed metal skies threaten a trailer park
of twenty shoebox forts eyed with mean windows.
Telephone wire grids cage sentry trees
and the odd cactus with outstretched arms.
One road only leads away
up to the horizon through desert and canyons.

In the foreground dust and stones.
On a rusty boulder this thirtyish blonde
smiles with confidence at the photographer.
Her shorts and top so tight, exposing flesh
so pale and so much. Those blown out
soft parsnip legs, blue veined, must shimmy.
She may say, "Are you serious? Do I give a damn?"
Here is a six-legged spider playpen
where a sickly infant kneels in his own mess
pressing his small face into the netting.

This outpost has a torpid feel.
Dry heat and boredom rise from the paper.
Taken the year I should have been in Arizona
but stayed instead in the cool Kentish damp.
This photo flickers my interest in its strangeness.
I am distanced by what could have been.
By now this child must be an adult.
Has he escaped yet? And is her smile
still so sure and satisfied?

FLORIDA BEACH

Yesterday, Columbus Day, a termite mass of people,
today a long blond deserted beach
fringed by bleached shanties,
sea oats on faded boardwalks,
drifting dunes where lines
of headhunched pelicans glide.

Only a child comes
to fly a swooping, stained-glass butterfly kite
over an unprinted whiteness of shell-fine sand.
He steps backwards to the ocean
where stipplings of spindrift fret, retreat,
in fans of frosted glass ripples
holding quicksilver translucent fish
threading the shallows.

He passes a snowy egret stalking,
cross-gartered yellow,
dominie of the tide flats,
while ill-disciplined sandpipers
beak-stab the beach
and run from waves on clockwork legs.

This wet shore
expansively reflects sky alone
so the distant child approaching
seems suspended in the heavens,
Icarus floating,
fastened with his kite.

ON OCEAN AVENUE

They'll never stay there again. All fades.
Each year the bay tree uses up more sky.
Aware of lemon and orange tree roots
invading the well, they no longer care.
For sale, the house made of cinder blocks
where the Stars and Stripes sway and the mailbox
leans back from pale sand on the road.
Scent of citrus blossom overlays the salt air
while a popinjay fish-crow serenades
the palm arcade and the surf rolls
in jade sprays under brocade clouds.
Footsteps daily scrape the boardwalk
as pelicans fly over in dumb parade.
Now the house has its shades down.

FOUND FLORIDA FISH

Hogfish, Houndfish, Goatfish, Gag,
Triggerfish, Needlefish, Doctorfish, Shad,
Bonefish, Batfish, Toadfish, Drum,
Fiddlefish, Trumpetfish, Cornetfish, Grunt,
Pinfish, Soapfish, Weakfish, Snook,
Ladyfish, Butterfish, Cutlassfish, Wick.

Snorer, Croaker, Crappie, Skate,
Shortnose, Bigeye, Warmouth, Scamp,
Bullhead, Sheephead, Look Down, Trunk,
Hairtail, Flip Flap, Alewife, Jack.

Stargazer, Mutton Snapper,
Blue Runner, Sergeant Major,
Golden Shiner, Southern Puffer,
Hoarse Muffle, Grass Porgy,
Thread Herring, Silver Jenny,
Man-of-War and Windowpane.

Others got away, again.

PARIS, SUMMER

Exhaust heat drains the day.
White light scours pavements.
Stepping as in a dance
black ladies pass
carrying their umbrellas high,
ritual totems,
taking their own pools of darkness
through the bleached city.

Sun ricochets from concrete.
On the Peripherique
dense traffic stagnates,
engines moaning, fumes cloying.
Ahead, a girl's bare legs and feet
stick from a car window -
yesterday's dusty baguettes.
From a far junction
a motor cyclist emerges
rumbling and reels around the trucks,
carrying a tall cross before him.
Our engines fall silent.
His metal head bows.
We sanction these crutches
strapped upright before him.
He curves past
and the horns begin a great grieving
like wronged geese,
until the traffic moves again.

HAMMER BEAM ANGEL IN WYMONDHAM ABBEY

Woodworm bore through my cold feet
so my dust falls down sunlight shafts
onto penitents' bowed heads.
They're submissive, full of guilt,
wanting their sins overlooked.
But mercy is above this leaded roof
beyond our faded winter sky.
I can't cope with too much thought,
being laden with carved oak wings
and all my colours lost in time.
While I clutch my prayer scroll
my mouth and eyelids curve in hope.
These brothers of mine up here are all
six-footers, waiting for our wings
to creak and beat together as we rise.

I look down on Norman arches in the nave,
sculpted traceries, mouldings, frets
and strawberry leaves. There were once
frescoes of flowers, beasts in a wood,
skeletons and three fat figures on a cloud.
I watched the kneeling paupers, Eligia
and Ester exchange rings below the pew.
Their favoured, flaxen child was mine, I felt.
When the old king passed I saw his faults
and virtues through his thin bones.
The space between us as a world's breadth,
the perspective of a spider in a cobweb.

Through the glass I see a changing cavalcade
outside, so dizzying. Light-headed,
yet with no fear of falling, I keep watch.

RISKY TICKING AT THE CORE

Footless bird flutters.
This heart hops in its cage
with unsteady hammer blows.
Dancing time is past.
Keystone no longer stout.
Blood torrents slow
to a seepage
through dark red valves.
Gnarled old ball of secrets
tries to repeat its refrain,
stumbles and shakes,
a tumbler sensing danger.
Stunts and twists pull bones
in their bleak rooms.
It's a guide, a knotted fist
punching a way out
of the broken home.

SINGING OWL

That solemn metal bellman
no-necked owlet
perches with flapper's legs
on an iron hat.
In daylight he sings silently,
his phoney mouth a fat circle.
He waits to jump in the air
when I'm not looking.
Wants to flex and clap
those tiny wings.
His hooked bill is anxious.
That flexible head won't rotate,
won't make warning snores.

He listens with ornamental
ear tufts for the sound
of a tin vole chewing nails.
Waits for night to regurgitate
pellets of brass bones.
Mesmerises moths which would
mob him to the candleflame.
No-one makes owl broth of him
for whooping cough.
He roosts in my skull hollows
wailing his low-pitched plaintive song.
He hunts in my sleeping darkness
pouncing and ripping my dreams apart.

UNPREPARED

At once the black bull fills the doorway.
Massive, snorting bulk. Hoof clatter.
The matador, washing up, turns at the din
relearns gut-wrenching fear, thinks
briefly of his suit of lights at the dry cleaners'.

This coffee-scented cupboard of a kitchen
is full of urgent animal stench.
The bulging-muscled monster, hate-fuelled
lolls out a foaming tongue, shudders,
bellows, spatters dung on the white tiles.

The matador in his glasses and striped apron
his dripping, empty hands held high, entreats
grabs a pickle fork and backs down the steps.
Charging, the bull bundles itself after him
into the yard, spraying sweat from his hide.

The man vaults low railings. Head up
the bull roars. Head down, batters bars.
Now the matador stabs his fork into the brute.
Water gushes out. The bull drops to his knees
puts his head gently against the man's chest.

As the beast crashes to the wet concrete
traffic roars by. The matador returns
to his kitchen, cleans and polishes his fork tines
hangs up his apron, walks out of his house
leaves the tap slowly dripping blood.

WET DAY DANCING

Slippery minnows of rain
dive into puddles.
It's raining fish; sharp and slithery.
A herring slides, gleams
into Sadie's camisole.
Wet and cold, it kisses
her flesh, dissolves to nothing.
In a downpour of pipefish
she dances on the pavement
face uptilted to the silver taste.
A shoal of sprats flickers past.
Small dabs plip down, fizz, expire.
Under a broken gutter she is caught
by a deluge of infant sturgeon
thrashing through her hair
with shining scales.
The shower stops. She turns
and turns, the lacy petticoats
flaring out, cascading tadpoles
on the flagstones.

BOOKS

Books are unlocked
boxes of treasure.
The key is the library.
Its shelves are stocked
with tragedy, comedy
and mystery.
Unending pleasure
for leisure.

VIEWING THE ANTIQUES PEOPLE

See the tallboys, simple lowboys, dumb
waiters, ornate or plain conforming
secretaries, smart dressers, plenty
       of fine whatnots.

Some display their well-upholstered seats,
overstuffed, immense padded ones, some
circular, some swivelling. There are
restored balloon backs, waved aprons, shaped
skirts. Secret, adjustable drawers
       are extended.

They have scrolled or thin tubular arms,
outcurved shell knees, splayed squat legs, solid
bulbous turned legs with rusticated
sabots. There are great hairy paw feet,
and massive club feet terminating
       in tasselled toes.

Some are distressed, even slightly glazed
or crazed, off their rockers, some damaged,
in poor condition, early or late,
originals, well decorated,
highly painted, and some of them are
       even stripped.

A few show dummy hanging bowfronts,
false exteriors, large Queen Anne chests
or small flat tops. Some are known to expose
       their reproduction parts.

ISABELLA'S MODERN POT

I had a great big flower pot.
Nothing did it hold,
But some dead and dusty herbs
And a ring of mould.

One night a vicious vandal
Broke in to burgle me.
But I took his head off with my axe
And potted it you see.

I covered it with a compost,
And watered it a lot.
And now I've flowering Basil
In my terracotta pot.

LEARNING TO LIKE MY SLUG OF AIR

This time next year
my sad gift plant which has
small white flies milling
round it will be dead
or it may have turned
into an insect-eating shrub
that smells of sick.
It stands next to the loud
radiator which will probably
be making the same
wailing noise it makes now.
The gas man said it was caused
by a slug of air.
This may be a vacant
mournful thing inside the pipes
calling for its mate.
No unplugging leech
will bleed it into silence.
This time next year
I may have learned
to like it.

THIRSK

That's it. The name I want
for myself. Singular. Just the one
epithet. Northern place, named by Danes.
It's terse, has a thickset tone
a strength to it, a quality
of thrift, of throng, of thrash and thresh
is stubbornly thrawn.
There's a thrust about it, a force
I like, a prickly thistlish note.
Seems in the throes of craving - thirst.
But, before all else, certainly sounds first.
First things Thirsk. From Thirsk to last.
I want to be Thirsk-rate
always in the Thirsk person.
A rebirth like an oath, emphatic.
It's a fizgig, a small firework
flirtatious with a fist.

Anyway, I don't need to justify it.
Just call me Thirsk.

Acknowledgements are due to the editors of the following publications in which some of these poems first appeared: The Rialto, The Shop, The Frogmore Papers, The New Writer, Literary Review, Oxford Magazine, Leviathan Quarterly, Spiked, Spokes, BBAC anthology, NWC anthologies, Reactions 1, 2 and 3, Ver Poets anthologies, The West in her Eyes, Tears in the Fence anthology, Waiting for the Echo, Exeter anthology, Biscuit anthology and The Forward Book of Poetry 2004. A sequence of stepmother poems won the Writers Inc Writers of the Year competition 2002.